THE VISITOR

Jane Borodale has an MA in Site Specific Sculpture from Wimbledon School of Art, and has written and exhibited work for a variety of sites including the Foundling Museum, London, and the Wordsworth Trust, Cumbria. She lives in the West Country with her husband and two children.

By the same author:
THE BOOK OF FIRES, a novel

Visit:
www.janeborodale.com
www.wealddown.co.uk

JANE BORODALE

The Visitor
A fiction in four strands

isinglass

First published in 2010 by Isinglass

Printed and bound in England by
CPI Antony Rowe, Chippenham, Wiltshire

A CIP record for this book is available from the British
Library

ISBN 978-0-953-32734-8

FSC
Mixed Sources
Product group from well-managed
forests and other controlled sources
Cert no. SGS-COC-002953
www.fsc.org
© 1996 Forest Stewardship Council

Kindly supported by The Leverhulme Trust
and the Weald and Downland Open Air Museum

The Leverhulme Trust

for Jennifer Hayes

ACKNOWLEDGEMENTS

These stories were written whilst Leverhulme Artist in Residence at the Weald and Downland Open Air Museum in Sussex. I am grateful for the generous support of The Leverhulme Trust who funded both the residency and this publication.

It was a privilege to have had access to the distinguished collection at the Weald and Downland Museum. I would particularly like to thank director Richard Harris for his support and enthusiasm; history associate Danae Tankard for friendship, discussion and so patiently sharing her expertise on the history of individual buildings; Julie Aalen, Roger Champion, Jonathan Roberts, Julian Bell, Diana Rowsell, John Procter, Bob Holman, Carlotta Holt, Hannah Tiplady and many other staff, volunteers and visitors for the warm welcome and knowledge that they so readily extended.

Thanks also to the West Sussex Records Office, Northampton Shoe Museum, Sheila Pearson, Joan Self at the Met Office, Jon Hill, Valerie Hill, John Donald and Sean Borodale.

CONTENTS

1

Deserted medieval village of Hangleton

THE EXCAVATION

You are expecting someone.

For some time now you have been looking towards the brow of the hill. The sky is thin with loss of light, and the descending air is cooling, condensing into dampness on your skin with the lateness of the hour. And then at last, as if from a great distance, you can just make out the shape of a man coming down the slope, moving on the pale whiteness of the path that straggles down like roots or fingers across the vastness of the grassy Down. And a woman behind him, his wife? You blink, and there's a child behind her, perhaps a small son, lagging behind as though the journey has been long and dull for his legs. You see him wander away from the path and he picks up something at his feet; a stone, a stick. And when the wind from the sea stops its blowing, you hear the woman's faint, winding hum of song that twists and shivers a little way towards you across the expanse and lapses again. Who are the dead?

They've come down Round Hill from Saddlescombe way. You see the dots of sheep drifting away from them as they pass through the flock. They're closer now, crossing the unploughed lynchets, skirting the striped squares of crops that you know to be blue flax, rye, Rivet's wheat, vetch – coming into the village. You see that the man and woman have empty baskets on their backs, and that the woman scuffs her foot as though her shoe has broken on the flinty road. And then they pass the longhouse and stop at the closed door of a cottage, low into the ground like a clam, with jumbly walls of flint and a thickly jutting gable. The roof is hard to see clearly in the greying light – there is a darkness to it that could be a thatch of reeds or old straw, though it could also be slate. The man unloops something from about his neck, then bends to the door with his back towards you and the door opens onto another kind of darkness and he is gone. At the entrance the woman turns back and calls the child with a shrill cry and soon the smoky coils and blusters of a new fire begin to unwind freely above the roof ridge, and the single shutter is lifted from inside and propped up, like an eyelid.

WOMAN: 'If life is heat running in the veins, then death claiming a body is like an ember's glow cooling to ashen cold. Prayers though can keep the thought of the souls of the dead warm in our heads; like raking the embers into the midst of the hearthstone and capping them over with the firecover for the night. Such is the power of words, when they're strongly intended, and we should mind what we say. Our own firecover is made of clay. I bartered for it roundly from the pedlar that clanked his way up to every door last year whether he was wanted there or not, because of what had happened the year previous with the moths' eggs all laid up inside the lengths of russet. That had looked like cloth at a good price but if we'd have known we would never have touched it. You can't see forwards though, can you, only behind and wisdom's all very well but it doesn't always strike. It was Lent time, he should never have been up here making us hanker after nice bits of russet when good plain falding cloth or hodden grey should be enough for any woman to be stitching garments out of.

"'It was no fault of mine," the pedlar kept hissing, wringing his hands all stained with something I suppose walnut juice or dirtiness, and then old widow Herdman threw a shoe at him and he didn't do the last two cottages but went off all puffed up with crossness and dragging his handcart back up the hill again where he'd come from or where he was going to, with its four wheels squeaking like buzzards under the weight of what he'd not sold.

'He'll be back next year if he's spared to live another – if any of us are. Time goes on with us wearing ruts in the track, smoothing the handles of tools with use, wearing our clothes out without a pause and needing new ones it can't be helped once they're quite past mending. A new bit of woollen cloth is a stake worth holding and laid up by good wives in better times, but the moth grubs had hatched before anyone noticed they were there, and inside a month they'd ate up the russet into gnawed-up tatters that fell apart like greens rotting in the pigpen, which made widow Herdman's heart bleed to see it, and the lord knows she could ill afford to be spending on new cloth like that; she scarcely able to find a smoke-farthing to pay the church at Pentecost just two months later. The pedlar's firecover though has gone on longer, and each night it keeps the day's fire just alive for the next; like a remembrance or dream of its own vitality, ready to burst into flames with a bit of coaxing and kindling at daybreak. That's how it should be with tending souls, too, keeping them warm in people's heads though they're dead and gone, even though come the Last Judgement it'll make no difference how they fared, prayer-wise.

'At least with the curfew on, there is no sparks.'

Forty years pass. Whatever else you're not sure of, there's a strong smell of baking bread.

GIRL: 'It's like being almost underground here, with the back of the house dug into the white bone of the hill. On a wet day in winter, with the rainwater puddling chalky outside the door mother jokes that it's like being buried alive. But her laugh is like nightjars as she says it, chirring in her throat – like the ground itself is speaking with its own grass stalks rubbed together, and her eyes are big and black like the nightjars' are, and wrinkled at the corners from getting up all night to see to babies, she says. They are unlucky birds but no matter as we scarcely hear them out this way except on a hot night in August, and for the rest of the year we've got the sound of mother chuckling inside herself and remembering things all over in her head as though there was no-one else upon this earth to turn up matters from the past, as the plough turns the earth. She likes to think about what's gone on hitherto and latterly, and of ways to be more careful as you're getting on with life and making do, and keeping your prayers firm inside your head as you go about. The baby's just newborn; too young to listen to her all day long and both my brothers are working out with father and so she speaks her mind to me, on and on.

'"Have to bring your children up right when you get wed," she says, "mindful of God as of the Devil."

'Mother's always looking backwards, poking at things already happened to make sure it was done right, finding it funny and yet not up to scratch. She points her finger at me and adds something else, as if she was having a new thought just come to her though I've heard her say it sixty times. "Anything you do as they're growing up will act on children in some manner, like a potter's thumbprint in wet clay."

'Father lives by the day, by the sun. He makes choices quickly and when he speaks people listen to him and do just what he says. "Now is the time to get those sheep penned up over the barley ground." "Today we'll bring in the beets from the south field." "The rain'll keep up all morning so we'll get that yoke looked over in the barn and ready for ploughing." "I can smell thunder so let's get those pigs in before they're skittish." My brothers think like that too – throwing up a tool into the air just to catch it now and again, working hard as dogs, asleep in a clap at night-time soon as the candle flame's blown out, and with no dreaming.

I dream all the time.

I like to think ahead of us.

I like the thought of what might go on sometimes before we've even got there, before we've put our meddling fingers all over things and changed the way they are, or would have been.'

A winter passes.
A summer.
A winter.

'Father has a knife with the letter 'S' beaten on the blade sideways in a base kind of metal that catches the firelight when he's carving spoons from a bit of beechwood. It was his father's before he died and perhaps the smith made it as a fancy; on a day when there wasn't much on in the way of shoeing oxen. Mother says it's nothing but the image of a snake and we should never keep it in the house as no good could come of anything that takes the Devil's semblance. Father's face shifted into the way he wears it when it looks as though the rain will start up before jobs are done. "It's for the family name, woman. I won't have no ignorance on that matter," he snapped, and for once she kept her mouth shut, though I could see unquiet twitching at the ends of her fingers as she pushed more charcoal into the fire under the pot.

'But sure enough, there came a hot day near to St John's when the Devil, smelling its own image lying idle across a dish, sidled right into the house in the shape of a viper, after the men had been shifting the stump of the old strawstack against the longhouse for Gilbert the reeve, and had likely disturbed it. Mother was out in the yard picking peas into the bushel tub.

'I felt it there more than I saw or heard it, though the length of its body made a sneaking, dry sound on the rushes as it glided a small way in over the threshold like a rippling, spoked shadow. It advanced into the chamber, then stiffened its head up and seemed to listen hard, as if to get the measure of our weaknesses. Its tongue zigged in and out, tasting the fire smoke, and then it turned and wormed its poisonous little self back out and thank God it did as the baby was right down there on the floor halfway between us, smelling all buttery and warm and soft of flesh no doubt to the Devil in that kind of form. He would have sunk his teeth in. I scooped up my sister and stamped my feet together on the ground to see him off. Then I went out the back and shouted for mother, and what I think of here was that there was a strong green smell of trodden nettles, because when you've been sore afraid it is the strange small things that you remember. When mother got her breath back from running she said it was a sign and that if we did not keep that knife out of this house we would rue the day. Some peas rolled out as she let go the tub and then she squeezed the baby tight and kissed the plumpness of her fingers like she was eating them. "He likes to take babies, when no-one's looking, when their mothers might be out at the back of the croft, or gone down in the salting season for a bit of work by the sea," she whispered fiercely at me, like she was spitting.

'The Devil doesn't like fish, especially not mackerel.

'Too cold, with a slippery force in the water and never once shutting its flat eyes, even later once netted and sizzling in the pot's fat and making your mouth water if you've been out picking flax all day with only a dry bit of maslin bread at noon to keep your belly quiet enough to finish up by sundown. Mackerel is too clean for him, from being in water and too close to God by half, especially of a Friday when all of Christendom, if it's not beggars, has its forearms covered in scales up to the elbow and a stubby knife hooking the guts out into a dish for keeping the cats sweet against rats: and there's a deal of rats down there, at the very coast. A mackerel's got a golden glazy eye that still looks out at nothing even when its flanks are broiled to a juicy crisp. It's as though it was looking right through you, at all the secrets piled inside. It would be hard to eat it with a guilty conscience pricking at you: that's one reason why the Devil is afraid of fish.

'My eldest brother made me a necklace out of fishbones when I was about eleven summers into life and starting to like to wear a thing of beauty about myself; little white ones smooth as moonlight on baby's teeth and sewed up on a bit of leather left over from making harness that was still biddable enough to get the cord through. He said it was no charm or else mother would have made me take it off, but I knew its luckiness was born of all the good fishing caught off Shoreham for which I prayed a deal of nights my palms squeezed together lest the northeast wind blow the boats out too far across the sea and over the edge.

'The sea's edge is just out of sight, so that even a wary fisherman could never be ready for it if the current were to drag his boat there, even on a clear day bright enough to see from here across the glittering stretch to the bill of Selsey and back, which is the furthest I can see though I've heard of London and how if you go there you could die inside three days from the bad air and the sheep's milk not being fresh. And abruptly caught out on the very brink a fisherman might teeter and shriek terribly like a sea raven, throwing his oars up, and then he'd be gone quick as slipping over a weir, to goodness knows, mother says the lower regions, where the Devil goes back to when he's done with causing trouble for a while, or if he has steaming wounds to lick where the strongest angels have fought him with swords. Father says it's just seaweed, but I think you can smell the brimstone sometimes, in a breeze off the sea.

'When they say that fishermen have got drowned – that's where they've gone; been quite dragged down, which is why the corpse never gets washed up down on the shore by the salt mounds where they do the boiling, so that there's nothing for wives to bury. Mother says it's the will of God even though it makes widows out of young wives alike as old, but I don't see how it can be when it's the Devil himself that's pulling them over.

'One thing I've seen is that a mackerel has in the pattern of its skin something of the sky and sea at once – so there is at least one creature in the world that marries up two sorts of element. I find that a comfort, two outside qualities lying side-by-side within a living body. Marriage too is a kind of doubleness – two overlain and making one. It'll be like that in my marriage when I am alive and wed, if the lord allows it, and I can't take a husband without his licence. It was not so long ago that there were Lord Poyning's men up here from the manor, ducking into the cottage doors all along the lane and breaking our own good querns we had with a lump hammer they'd brought on purpose. Mother cried out that it was a pity and a waste of a family man's

17

tools what they were doing but they said we should have seen it coming, what with getting too baulky and above ourselves. Now we have to take the wheat and barley down to his mill to be ground and leave him what he calls the proper charge in kind, when we want flour. He'd have a share out of our lifeblood if he could, and he may yet. Trouble on the hill, his men call us up here, with hardly enough sheep to call a flock. Not like Patcham with two thousand out on the open Down.

'After the marriage at the church door there'll be dancing and Richard the wait will play his whistle, and there'll be cakes, and that night my new life will begin, as one half of a piece of wholeness blessed by God. There's two halves to everything, of course. When I say what I think about my hopes for when I'm wed, mother chuckles more, as though I were a half-wit, but when I ask her why she says it's because I've got stocky ideas and shouldn't have, about how men and women should live along of each other.

'She looks down at the ring on her finger and smiles in a way I do not understand. "Never did know where father laid his hands on that," she says, turning it about, so that I can see the band of naked paleness on her skin beneath it.'

The finger ring is silver gilt, strands of metal skilfully twisted and beaten to shape. Try it on – look! The ring fits your forefinger as if it was made for you. One minute passes. While you are wearing it, can you feel what a minute was like, when time was passing almost seven hundred years ago? Such small measures of time put end-to-end together make a long rope – that is the way we have agreed we will arrange it in our minds, on paper, and its singular continuity makes something simple out of something infinitely complicated.

"'Isn't it a fine thing for a girl to have hopes and dreams to look towards?" I ask my mother, then I add something I would never have thought to ask before, when I was younger: "Your own life here with us surely hasn't been so bad, as father's wife." The words come out blunter than I mean them, and louder too, like hammering. Daughters can be hard on mothers.

'And she screws her eyes up very tight when I say that, as if the weather was getting into them a moment, and then she looks as if she's already thinking of something else and goes back to stringing up onions.

"'It's the smoking of fish that causes it to last a long while, not the length of the life itself," she says unexpectedly, over her shoulder.

"'What do you mean, Mother?" I ask, and stop my stirring. I wait to hear what she has to say above the whine of the northeast wind, which is the one that cuts you right in two.

"'Tend to your soul as you tend to your fire," she just says, plainly, without any laughing — like they did in the sermon in church a Sunday ago, and the ring flashes out a soft gleam as she puts her hand rustling into the basket for another clutch of onions. The pot bubbles undisturbed as I watch how a spider hangs spinning in the light, then dabs one fine long leg out and goes on falling on its strand. They say a lot of things in church, interlarding the useful bits with words I don't understand, and it makes my knees ache, standing still for

19

so long. Father was asleep back home for that sermon, as he'd been up all night with the ewes in lamb, but I know what he'd have said about that afterwards if he'd have heard it, how it was not proper use of a man's time. "As you tend to your fire" is all through the day, and surely that can't be right, thinking inwards like that in such a quantity. Not when there's so much to be done. I scrape the mash to stop it burning in the bottom of the pot and when I look up the spider has plumbed to the floor and disappeared. What could go wrong if I weren't to tend things with so much attention? There's nothing to be frightened of about what's out there ahead of us. It's only that mother's always imagining there to be sin and its consequences: she makes a joke of it, her black eyes crinkling up like stones are being thrown into pools, but I know she is afraid of what might follow on the heels of anything.'

April.
May.
June. The battle of evening lingers long in this month, but the dark wins in the end, the light struggling on until it gives up for the night when the bell at St Helen's strikes the curfew. You can just hear it ringing still, though the sound and the shape of the bell itself has changed over time.

OLD MAN: 'Not many notice an old man like me, trudging late up the lane on my way back from mowing come haytime. It's eventide in mid-June, and the sun no longer even a foxy smear of pinkness above the bare hill. Last one up from the field as I'm wont, neck itching from hayseed and my throat dry as old leather and looking ahead to something from the jug when I've got home. Crickets chirping in the grass all the way, especially when I pull up to rest when my breath's coming a bit raspy going uphill. Sickle's on my bent back and can't see much where I'm stepping as the light's half gone, but I can make out the humps of beehives and I can hear bees humming a thousand-fold inside. Busy time of year, though not like harvest. There's a fair bit to worry about – yields these past few harvests being that low that there's been fool's talk of ploughing up the sheep pasture come January, but it'll never hold grain up there – too clayish and flinty for growing much of anything, and that talk'll come to nothing. Down here along the village there's hearthsmoke everywhere tonight and not a drop of wind above the roofs. My walk home's mostly the same as it always was since boyhood but with changes between seasons fleeting along, and I've been doing boon work if I like it or not down there for these forty-three years if anyone's counting and I'll doubt they are, since God saw fit to take my wife from me, and it would seem most others think in measures of ale instead of numbers. I'm not saying I don't neither, not when it's mortal hot like it was at noon. But that as it may, this evening as I get past the hives, there's one thing different from the same spot yesterday. There's a small boy stood unmoving in the lane before me. He has his face turned up to the dimming sky and his hands outstretched – all pale in the gloom, and the air about him is thick with white moths.

'Can't see the boy's face, but I know who it is from the stink of his riveling shoes made with raw skin. And in the gloom I can see that the darkness of his mouth is open in wonder, like he's seeing a vision. When I greet him he startles like a cony and turns and runs as though he should have long ago been getting back. The quick pad of his feet on the dry track sounds almost hollow and then above the croo and cluck of fowls settling behind the palisade at the yard's edge, in the distance I hear a cott door creak and slam shut. I picture the boy squatting down at the hearth by the living flames, folding his knees up, his heart racing. His sister is there too by the fireside, spooning out a sticky broth of worts and barley into bowls. If she'd only look at him closely, though no doubt she won't, she might see that his bony face is shimmering with dust from the moths' wings; a dark silvering as though he's been touched by spirits, the little rascal.

'I've forgot how much of a thirst I'd had on me.

'Out here in the lane the furry whiteness of the moths' flight is all about and I'm feeling an ache, like there's an old uncomfortable dog turning and settling down again inside my chest.

'The souls of the dead are crowding the air at night in summer, drawn to the warmth near dwellinghouses, like ghost moths to the smell of honey, or suckle bush, or other sweet flowers.'

Thirty years go by now, and a night mist begins to creep up and clutch at the fissures of hills, like the sea's own dream of reclaiming the land. Indeed it does not seem so long before the marginal seaboard; the coastal stretch where the women boil salt on mounds and gather shellfish, is beneath the lapping edges. You know that it is a unexplained loss noted in accounts across the south, as the sandy, stony littoral appears to be shrunk by the sun and blown away by the breeze.

OLD WOMAN: '...Or blown away by God's own breath. We ceased taking the creels down last year as there was woeful fighting over what was left to pick and so much disturbance at the coast between the oyster rakers that a woman could come back emptyhanded, especially of a spring tide. The skirt of land has slipped beneath the sea's edge, no-one knows why, nor how long it'll be before the water gains its way right up the hill and drowns us in our sleep. Sometimes when I wake in the pitch black at night I can smell salt in my hair. There are things afoot. God has sent us bad weather and bad crops, the sheep are dropping dead of a murrain and now the fish creels stay home unused with nothing going into them. My good neighbour stores her hen's eggs in one, because she won't let a thing of service go to waste.'

Two years pass.

'And if she had lived it would've broke her heart to see the state of life we live in now. I cannot remember what it is to prosper.'

BOY: 'Before the feast of St Matthew was when it started. The pestilence entered the cottages down near the rector's house at first and everyone prayed for the sick. It was a warm, wet summer we'd had. Nobody knew then what evil it was that had come amongst us, and then at once there began to be something about the slant of the sun in the sky that was not right, and it was like when a blight of rot hits the stored-up fruit and the whole crop is lost with no warning, oozing wetness and sour stink, white with maggots. That's how it came. Up the lane as quick as spilling something and smelling it, and my sister was gone, then Mammy was gone. I'd heard her say how after death there was a mingling of more than one quality easy enough in the ground; she gripped my fingers like a dry vine as she breathed it out as if she wanted to take me and I jumped back in fear with my heart beating and went to fetch water. When I came back to her she was dead with her black lips open a crack like she'd gone on without me but was still calling.

'Now it's Father there on the pallet. He won't swallow morsels. On his back, a murrey-coloured mottle spreading over his face and words spilling from his mouth in gibbered loops like the guts are coming out of him already and then he coughs himself quiet and spits up blood and slimy humours into a cooking pot that I empty into the ditch beside the house. And when I stand outside I see that every aspect of the world is changed and that by the door the unpicked brambles and the elderberries are part of a greater blackness rotting and dripping in the bushes, soaking into the land. It was the end of harvest when it came – did we not give thanks for what we had? Much of the grain was got in already, but then those who were well enough to reap what was left had to tend to the sick and it stands buckling and mouldering in the fields now as though forgotten, like a careless husbandman's mistake. The fields are crawling with rats and starlings, gorging themselves sick on our ill-luck. I do not look out at the glare from the sea.

'Jackdaws fill the empty house in front of us, squabbling amongst themselves like a heartless gang, pitching in and out where there's nobody left to shut the window, spattering the sill.

'Nobody steps over our unswept threshold once his body is taken; even the quit-rent has gone uncollected. I am cold now. There is nothing but a chill in the wool of this coat, as though something old is drawing me down to itself, clutching me to the cold black pool at the bottom of its well. My soul... Some people from here took off and went up over the hill northwards, and whether they died on their way to a clean place no one from here will ever know.'

Fifty years pass. Perhaps there is someone inside the house now and perhaps there is not. And then you see how the house slowly heaves itself inward – crumbling walls, crushing pots with its own weight of rubble, the inexorable slip of matted, greening thatch. Once the roof has collapsed then plants crack the earth open at the hearth with their growth. At first only mosses ameliorate the sharpness of edges, and then frost, wind, animals, lack of heed begin to flatten the place as it was, into its own concealment.

But nowhere are the dead more apparent than in a deserted village. Their presence by their very absence fills the sinking hollows of what is left. And it is the absence that wears away at the signs of occupancy, year by year, until the ground is closed again, though leaving a mark as when two sides of a old wound have healed.

Under that skin are the buried pieces, bits of bones, particles, stories. You cannot hear any of the way they speak – we can only blindly examine what is dug up later and take turns to make guesses with degrees of authority, to make lists:

the corroded knife with the letter S worked into the blade

the ox shoe

the sherd of green-glazed jug

the bag of brown nails like rusty cloves

the blackened tiles

the finger ring

the iron key eaten away by the soil to brittleness

the yellowed fishbones

the silver penny of Edward the Third

the linen smoother.

What is most lost to you is all that is fleeting, impalpable; kisses, passions and dullnesses inside a man's heart, leaps of faith, the gaps of waiting, breathing, the beating of blood in the veins. And what else is known to you is just a tangle of names on vellum: Spring, Slengbody, Slezbody, Smothe, Stighelman, Smale.

2

Bayleaf: Wealden house from Chiddingstone, Kent

LAST

'We're raising the shape that describes the space of a dwelling; two carpenters, with axe and brace and mallet, and boys dropping wallthreads as bidden, chalk-marking where the cuts should go, holding the shearlegs, the nail box. It's all about bearing, stress and balance. The timber-frame, the green oak bones of a place, is cut from a place in the Weald nearby, by hewers and sawyers who bring it on the cart, squared up in the forest. The stripped bark goes to the stinking tanners, the brash and loppings go for charcoal. Nothing gets wasted – anything that comes to pass has a use found for it. Drive a stake into the ground; a bird will light on it soon enough.

'This new house we're rearing is like a ship in massiveness, hefty arch braces taking the pull of the tie-beam above the hall, and the hips of its jetties opening up the space to the sun at the upper storey. There's a prospect up and down the scoop of valley, and a sense of its own fields about it. It's a fine standing for a house – good pasture, pannage, underwood. It's a good house to work on. I'm preparing broad doors with clicket latches. Wall-posts and wall-plates. Mortices. The back-and-forth chewing of the handsaw's edge is like a neat, determined dog's bark. There's a squeaking knock as two halves of a joint pull together when the peg is struck into them, and it eases in like a tight sort of butter. The peg is seasoned, and the joint is green and cut out of kilter by a half-finger's width so that as it shrinks it knits up like a bone setting. You smell the character of cut oak here in your jaw, and its warm body vinegarness. I feel right working wood with my two hands, breathing the wood-smell, chipping out with a sharp gouge, briskly, the chock, chock of the mallet almost a sound inside my arm as inside my skull, like the mallet's a wooden end to my own arm. Above the buttery in the south-east corner of the service bay I've done a handsome bit of sparring off the dragon-beam like an ear of wheat, and those joists should hold a hundredweight without flinching. I like working both the dry unyielding wood and the green wood that bears leaf. A year for every inch we say it takes to fully dry, planks stacked in the yard with sticks between, and oak's not always good for boards, it'll twist and kick up a nail if it wants to. Oak is wilful – you can't tame it, only put its strengths to use. I like its tabby marks when quartersawn, and the silvery cast the skin of the wood takes on with aging.

'Who'd be a fleshmonger dealing in death and dripping, decomposing, when I can put up the bare bones of a living house in the time it takes a butcher to kill an ox and take it apart into pieces. That's the thing about wood – it's not a dead entity if it's treated right. No reason why it couldn't live for more than six hundred, eight hundred years? Not if it's heartwood. Not if the joints are sound, with good air moving about and the groundwork is level. It's a clean way to make a livelihood, whichever way you wend it.

'I'm paid enough to feed my family more than beets more than boiled meal and pigroot, but they've a big mouth between them and I need to count on my health, my strong thumbs for weal and prosperity. Nothing's sure in this world nor the next, not for carpenters, roofers, daubers, no-one. Look at my hands spread out; the fingers are thick like roof spars and my forearms more like beech limbs than flesh my wife says, and as close-grained being in my prime. And storms and droughts, lean seasons and happinesses have been compressed into rings about my own heart since my own first spring.

'My wife will have white herring on the table when I've lain the tools down at sundown – and may that last another twenty-year. Did I say what are the tools we use? Rulestone, wimbells, forpices, dryvel, twortsaw, handsegh, addice. Did I say what the enemies are? Rot, fire and beetles. But mostly the wood we have hewn for the principal timbers, such as collar and purlins, is heartwood. The beetles can't get there; it gladdens me lying abed in my own place and hearing them clicking away in the sapwood, because I know the core of the oak is too tough for them, too dense where the sap doesn't run, it's nearer to stone, stronger than they are. It's like war that I'm winning when I use heartwood, and oak is more than a rough king, it's a whole kingdom even a god almost, among trees.'

A hundred years later an old woman lies infirm in bed, and there is a young girl sitting by her, stitching at a red-dyed woollen tunic in her lap, sucking her thread and tilting her work into the morning light.

'You're not listening,' the old woman grumbles. 'I'm telling you about the old days and you're missing it. Here!' She raises herself with difficulty and points to a dark mark on the beam above the bed. The mark is long; too firm to be a smudge, but has a fleetness borne of some kind of movement. Its brownness is the colour of the gills of horse mushrooms, and appears smooth with age and with being overlooked. 'See that? I'll bet you can't say what that is.'

The girl glances up and shrugs. 'Just a mark.'

'That's from the old days,' the old woman says again, as if it were proving something. 'That's from when life was hard, and full of stories.'

'How long ago?'

'Well…'

'Was the world black? That's how I think of it.'

'Dark with unknowing, you could say.'

'And was it very cold?'

'The past is always cold.'

'Like river water?'

'Colder than that.'

'Like iron?'

'As cold as iron lying outside in winter.'

'But there was fire, wasn't there?'

'There is always fire. It is too difficult to imagine how it was before fire came.'

30

'And that brown mark...' the girl narrows her eyes, 'is made by scorching.'

'You can see that now because you're looking at it clearly.'

'A flame was too close, that's all.' The girl shifts herself impatiently upon the bed.

'Fifty years ago a candle flame licked its brightness against the oak for a little too long and began burning its shape into the surface. But why? What small, neglectful moment caused its unattendance? That is the part that we don't know, or leastways I cannot remember.'

'Did you live here?' The girl seems surprised to think of the old woman when she was young. 'Did you have dark hair, plaited like mine? Was there a sheenness to it, like jackdaws?'

'Well, the north wind came from the north, if that's what you mean. And the onions grew fat shoots up from the ground and sometimes birds fell dead out of the sky. Twas ever thus. And yet...' She stops to cough.

'And yet what?' The girl's curiosity has woken up, and she puts her sewing down. 'How was it when you were younger? Before my father had been born, even.'

'There were differences.'

'Like...'

'Colours were brighter.'

'Colours?'

'The green of the leafy trees, the blue sky in May, the blood-red berries in December.'

'How could that be? How could they have been more so than they truly are? The world seems bold enough to me.'

'Because everything was newer then.' The thought

31

of it seems to have made the old woman cross. 'The colour of things was more upright then, more...' Her scaly, knobbled, birdish hands scrabble with the bedsheet as she searches for a word. 'More *utter*.' Her voice cracks as she says that, like her throat is made of something dry and rough, and the girl feels a jump of fright at the gaping oldness of her lying there in the bed, beneath the covers like a brittle length of rock, and she fixes her gaze instead on her own pink hands folded in her lap.

'That's right,' she hears the old woman going on, her words rasping out, 'the colours burst into your face like they had a heat to them. And especially when I was young, the year my heart was broken, did I find the colours were too bright to bear, so that I had to tip my face towards the earth, and keep in the shadows of the woods whenever I was out. Somehow the sunshine shining on my troubles made everything round me seem too strong. My husband said I was the palest girl in Chiddingstone by the end of August. In and out of the shaw collecting cherries, dry sticks for kindling, fungus too. There was one white puffball that was the very size and heaviness and softness of a baby's head. And tender as a baby's flesh to bite on once I'd sliced and fried it with lard in the pan. Its taste was something to savour, like the earth's own fish – I had a craving for fungus, three months away from being brought to bed with my third child, and big with it. But the smell of the infant I'd already lost that summer was strongly about me, a sweet, beeswaxy freshness that I'd catch on the air when I turned my head.

'When misfortune happened again the year after

that and my oldest boy too was taken from me, it wasn't so much that I was hardened to it, but that the grief of the first had taught me a way to get through the terrible sharpness and brightness that there is in the world. Now though there is a dimming of things. Because things fade as they get older, and the world itself is no exception; you'll find that out.'

There is a silence in the chamber, though outside in the yard the geese are making their clanking, bucket-handle noise amongst themselves. A light breeze runs through the open windows.

'But the dragonflies by the millpool!' the girl exclaims suddenly. 'Sunning their wings on the fresh reeds at the water's edge – the bluest blue you could ever dream of – bluer than kingfishers. They come crawling up the stalks, dragging themselves like dull little filthy dragons out of the dead-brown sludge of their very own past, into a bright world to be the brightest things in it. And everything makes itself new again, every year. It's what spring is for, surely!' The girl is almost offended at the idea that the world is fading. But now it is the old woman's turn to choose not to listen, or the fierceness of the memories have exhausted her and the girl thinks she may have fallen asleep, as her head is turned away so that she cannot see if her eyes are still open.

'And the mark on the wall,' the girl whispers, just in case. 'How did the mark come to be there?'

There is a creak of rope as the old woman turns in the bed.

'That bit of charring,' she begins, 'came from an ordinary night I was going to bed. I had climbed upstairs with the wick already lit − right here.' She gestures across the chamber. 'I pressed the wet clay against the crossbeam with the taper in it, and undressed quickly in its yellow light. My garments were damp at the hem, and cold as I pulled the wool over my head. In the cradle little Martha had kicked off her covers and as I tucked her back in, an owl whooed in the walnut tree outside, right close to the house and I shivered in my nightsmock in the chill to hear it, because an owl's noise can shake and tremble inside your own flesh while it's being cried out. That was when my husband Thomas called me downstairs to pull his boots off. "Mrs Wells! Mrs Wells!" That was how he shouted out for me. I daresay I took a blanket off the bed and threw it about myself as I went down the steps. His voice was odd, which was what drew me to him like I was flying. His boots were claggy with mud, and his hands too cold and shocked to get a grip at them. He told me news that night, how Tom Hayward and a loose, wicked woman from over Sundridge way had poisoned Joan his faithful wife to death with ratsbane. To death! My stomach turned itself over and over to hear it, he'd ate with us here at high table that many times. He a Christian man, and she died after Christmas. In my mind's eye I kept seeing his red lips, chewing on mutton after he'd said grace.' She hesitates now, as if unsure. 'Whatever the news or the timing of it, I must have forgot the flame burning on and on upstairs, making a mark.' She sniffs. 'Was I already in bed giving the baby the breast, did I fall asleep before blowing it out? Or was there just an uncommon draught that night between the window shutters, guttering the flame against the oak, and we'd not noticed?' The old woman cackles. 'Or were we early in marriage, before any child had come to us, and a passion of the flesh had left it alight, because that night he'd wanted to watch how I was beneath him as his lawful wife – for he was young then and the burden of superintending the land, the business of profit and loss with oats and wheat hadn't yet drained the lustiness from his self, as it did later. Rye, barley, dredge, vetches.' The old woman's smile wanes on her face. 'Or was it me at all, that gave rise to that mark? I'd doubt it matters.' And to change the subject she jabs a finger at the pewter jug on the form by the bedstead. 'Pour me some water.'

'To me it matters!' the girl retorts, tipping the jug too fast and spilling some. Like all youngsters she admires quickness and with the precision of youth, does not like the actualness of things about her to be crumbled. She is disappointed. She likes a story to be quick and supple and full of truth and proper remembrance – and to get to the sense of it crisply, like biting into a good apple. There was no satisfaction to be had in letting it all fall about you, hearing the meaning of the story rot away even as the words were being spoken. It felt like weakness, carelessness to lose the very spirit of what it properly was. She will never let herself do that, she decides, even when she is old. She has a sudden urge to get up and fetch the brush and start to sweep the floorboards clean. Yes, this afternoon she will get down on her hands and knees and scrub right under the bed and in all the corners. As if the girl has spoken aloud the old woman glares as she slurps at the rim of the cup, and there is a sharp glint in her eye that belies both her frailty and the confusion of her words.

'Or perhaps I was just sewing in bed because it was warmer there.' The old woman inches herself back on the bolster and looks up at the rafters. She does not trouble to wipe at the wetness round her mouth with her sleeve or the sheet. 'Lost in the diligence of my work like a good girl, stitching in and out, in and out with my bodkin flashing in the candlelight. You see,' she waits with a triumphant pause, and then snaps out, 'because you don't know, do you! Those being *my* memories.' And with a huff and a degree of difficulty she turns her back.

There are many things embedded in the fabric of a house. In the walls there is hair in the plaster, sieved lime, tallow, fingerprints, dung, tar, the sap of trees. Trodden or soaked into the earth floor there must be torn-off fingernails, drips from pots, blood, spit, bird-lime, dried-up liquids, dust, baby-spew, sawdust, fat, peelings, tears, ashes. There are bones and husks dragged by rodents into cavities, dropped-out feathers, cat fur, dead and living insects burrowed in the timbers, spores and dampnesses, particles driven into cracks by wind, and brought from miles away on boots, hems, hooves.

Occasionally, there can also be objects, planted purposefully. And it is hard not to hear the stepping of feet inside the house, once you know that a set of lasts was hidden there in the seventeenth century. Against the chimney breast in the upper chamber, between the bricks behind the daub behind the layers of plaster, their presence implies that another entrance to the house is always possible. Three wooden lasts for moulding shoes about – the foot's shape of a man, a woman, a child – a muddled row in a stopped-up hole facing the devil's blundering descent down the chimney when he comes. He has a raw, ugly thirst for shoes and homely trinkets and the souls they were attached to. The lasts are like the balls of bones but harder, thicker – like kernels, brown and dry and surface-dull with lack of use, and they tell you of an occupant's reasoned internal fierceness in the face of the unknown, which always arouses fear in times of greater darkness. Perhaps they are concealed when the Pigotts hold the lease of the house, a time of uncertainty when Charles the First rules without parliament, raking in taxes for ships that nobody wants, and mistrusts are brewing. For good measure other items are placed there too – a glove, a wooden spoon that will be eaten by rats, and a pair of man's shoes, worn out, with the heel and sole missing. We might now without effort or unease call the group set protectively against the chimney a spiritual midden; to confuse the devil with their smell and form of humans and trap his intent in the dead-end of the wall itself. But when in use, at the height of its purpose, nobody speaks of it – a wordless thing. Perhaps this is right, that we should never give voice to the stealth of fears tip-toeing through our nights, nor our defences. There is after all a strength in silence – and in keeping the ears sharp for the approach of danger.

'What are you doing?' the child asks the man who is mixing mortar beside the scuttle of bricks. Over the month the new chimney is growing by increments as each section dries and strengthens enough for more to be laid on top.

'Finishing up soon.' And the trowel rasps wetly as the man goes on working. His lips are powdery and grey with dust, but when he speaks the inside of his mouth and tongue look scarlet. The child fingers a rough brick. It is made of reddish local clay, dug and clamp-burnt nearby.

'But what is that?' the child points to something he can see behind the unfinished top course, halfway up the wall. He can't stop asking questions, because the building work is so discomfiting and fun. It still feels unnatural to be standing on boards where before the hall was open to the rafters. He likes to put his eye to the cool updraught of a crack between the new floorboards and look down at the movement in the room beneath, to make himself giddy. He can see the gleam of earthenware; a snail-brown pot, the dry, bushy herbs upended.

'Nearly done – will have got to the top by noon, and then I'll be down for a bit of bacon.' The man scratches his beard with a thumb caked in mortar. He doesn't mind children. He has three of his own and knows how to keep up half-talk as he works, his mind turning over other things.

'No, but that,' the child is more insistent now, pointing at something he can see poking out behind the line of bricks. 'That roundish thing.' He strains his head up to see.

'Just bricks, there,' the man says. 'Nothing in there. A hole, it is.' He ruffles the boy's hair as if to rub out the thought of what it was, and the boy thinks of making a little boat out of woodscraps and runs quickly off to find his sister because he has forgotten already and the sun is glinting on the millponds. And later, by the time he's done his weeding around the patch of cresses in the kitchen garden and helped to scrape the trenchers into the chicken-pail, the great red chimney breast is finished above the inglenook. The stack needs to be built outside to sit on top, and it will be weeks before it is all dry enough to light a fire against the new firedogs the ironmaster brought in readiness.

By Hallowmas the hall does not fill with smoke as soon as the fire is lit, for the first time in the history of the house. Two centuries of smoke have given a brown-blackened sheen to the upper walls, with the ripple of the wattle showing through like a dark hide, hairy with blackness. But the screens of the enclosed parlour are whitened over now behind the hanging cloths, like the shells of hens' eggs. The boy's grandfather is distracted by the chimney, and for the first few days during the newness of its use keeps getting up to go out and stand in the chilly yard with his back to the sunset, squinting roofwards at the eddy of smoke billowing, the sparks orange against the dusk.

'What are you doing, Granda?' the boy asks, trailing after him.

'Just checking the smoke's working the way they said it would, now the wind's got up.'

'It's cold Granda.'

'Beetle off inside, then.'

But John Pigott goes on gazing at the stack, getting accustomed to its protrusion, till they call him for supper. And in daylight it is a while before its long shadow cast on the sunny grass stops giving him a start of surprise on seeing it, just as a tall man's shadow would, falling

39

suddenly beside him.

Then the Rose family arrives, first Gregory and then William and his wife Mary who have eight children born to them here and two of them lost. And you find that there are always footsteps to be heard if you listen hard enough inside a house, or out. The pad and scuff of leather on floorboards or the spinning wheel's treadle, or the tap tap of hobnails, or the clack of pattens or clogs. Children's bare running feet across strewn field rushes or smoothed earth. A servant's shuffling weight creaking in the upstairs chamber as she tidies a bed. A carter's boot-scrape as he brings a butt of salted lobfish to the door. And there are always the traces left by footfall, the passage of someone's constant movement marking a place indoors so you can see the passing, like a green trail where a stockman has gone through the whitened grass of a frosty pasture, or the narrow baldness of a track where animals have made their way to a trough out of habit, the traces criss-crossing across a field when seen from an upper window.

But there are other consequences of footsteps. Man can be defined in an abundance of ways; by his speech, by his offspring, by his life's work, and yet nothing comes close to walking in the sense of making certain sorts of changes on his habitat. The patterns left by speech do not work away at the very substance of the place like walking does. Passing across a space many times over makes a man's path into his own familiar furrow along which his feet can carry themselves comfortably without thought but with a deepness of knowledge – between door and hearth, hearth and settle, up the steps, to the window, to the well, to the barn, the far field, the wood. And these passages between positions, these ways of being in a space become imprinted, threadlike, in a way that can be felt for centuries, and moving through them can give a tug, an elastic snagging, as though the body recognises change in the path's atmosphere, the clue of it. Why else would it be that you can move more fluently in one direction, while another way seems almost to resist your passing?

Throughout the eighteenth century, though, and then already into the beginning of the next, changes of tenant and a lack of consistency in husbandry and tillage have made a rattling, unsettled atmosphere inside the house. Just two years' incumbency each time or less, and it shows in the farmstead's state outside – the two ponds disused and silted up, just boggy patches with the reedy brook pouring through from the valley's head to toe. And the unrest is buried in the house in more ways than one, as they say that a cache of cutlasses and swords has been put behind the fireplace. It is for a confusion of reasons that you can't make out:

'It's the French,' someone says.

'I'll pray those blades have a keen edge put on them – the skin of Frenchies is as tough as boot-leather.'

'They'll be running all over us here, that bloody Napoleon waving his hat.'

'It'll be like hell's swept up from the Channel in his little boats.'

'He eats babies,' the dairymaid at Bore Place says, her eyes clear with fright.

Or is it because of the taxes, the year without a summer, the inexcusable cost of bread?

'Starving to death they'd have us.'

'Squeezing the blood out of us to oil their machines.'

'Saving them money.'

'Only the fat white miller making a profit out of grain we grew. On a quiet day I find there's nothing but the drubbing of that waterwheel going round.'

'May as well be grinding gold up between his millstones.'

'If there's riots they've got to take blame.'

'If a man gets up a group to defend theirselves.'

The house is sold in 1828 by auction in London.

Some, like John Smith of Ivy House leasing now from John Williams who made the purchase, know how a house can be defined by the fields around it.

'Lower Howletts, Little Pit Field, Long Brooms, Square Broom Shaw, Slip Shaw, Great Hooklands, Little Hooklands, Nine Acres,' he says, 'having their separate characters and value, but jointly they add up to much of what a house draws its life from. These fields evolve the year out for me, as though they soak up the vital point of every season and turn it to each use that they have. The Dane Field is pasture, with the dairy herd feeding on it, or steers. And Bridgers Field is among four acres one rood laid to hops: I'll have them twiddling the bines up the chestnut coppice poles, dressing the hills, pinching out pipeys, hoeing down alleys, cutting the bines with the dressing knife, picking the green hops into the bins and then off to the oast to cure. Those are

Golden Tips and Canterbury Grape this year. I don't live here, the house has been divided into tenements for labourers like Birchard and his wife, and Wardhorne and his lot and John Coomber, but I'm the kingpin, making decisions, commanding the seeding, sowing, reaping, picking. It all converges in my farmer's eye.

'And at evening in summer if you've laid the ground right there's that slack time — maybe a week — when there's nothing to do but stand back and admire the growing. Prodigious growth and greennesses of different hues in each field like they're all opening their palms out wide and saying, "take it!" "Fill up the granary!" "Stoke up the oast house furnace and loosen the sacks ready!" Makes your mouth water. Flax, furze, grain. I can stand at the window looking north up the valley and see a patchwork of arable colour winking on and off all year.

'But it's not like conjuring, this line of work, it's damn hard labour and heartache. Imagine you see a black flock of starlings coming down in the mead taking the ripe oats the day before harvest, stripping it to the bare nigh-useless fodder stalk. Imagine there's a turn in the weather and the clouds purple with hail and you're helpless against it, and the misery of the flattened corn after it's passed over you just can't relate to a man in a trade drawing on dead matter. Not a tailor, mending, making good out of a bad job, cutting a bit here a bit there, stitching things up. Not a blacksmith, putting his irons back in the fire to beat them again. When there's mildew there's mildew, say. Ruination. When a frost's blackened the early peas to death where they stand.

43

When cheeky damn children break into the barn and slide on good hay with their dirty legs messing it up. And it's raining cats and dogs down your collar for two hours and you've been up since four that morning, before the sparrows. Some nights I'm too stiff to bend to my own bootlaces, and filthy with it.'

The dairy herd at Bayleaf Farm is sold in 1922, comprising excellent cows and heifers, in calf and in milk (Snowdrop, Pretty Maid, Tulip, Ruby), steers and shorthorn bull (Ruth's Princeling), plus three milk-cart horses (Polly, Kitty, Peggy), and five fat pigs.

And the house itself is sold again in 1956, and in 1958.

'So much has happened here – picture the normality of it all. The radiators above the waxed parquet of the floor. The lagging round the watertank and pipes up in the roof-space. The pear tree in the hedge bearing a crop of small, hard pears. Wasps. The metal window jammed open a crack and the smell of jasmine drifting in. Grilling pork chops. Arguing. Being late getting children to school. Cutting the cake at a brother's wedding. Sitting on the garden bench by the back door, under the mauve of wisteria creeping slowly against the chequered bricks of the house, as though it had all the time in the world to reach maturity. Waiting for the snapdragons to bloom. Feeling the sun. Never foreseeing the compulsory purchase, the bulldozers, the lake brimming horribly at our feet like a bad dream and, after the demolishing, the water risen over the mashed earth and rutted tracks where the garden had been, the lane where my children played, the barns, the oast chimneys.

'East Sydenham Water say that the reservoir is an obligation of modern life, and in some ways it demolishes us too once the fight is over. It feels as though it is my spirit they have taken apart when the house comes down in pieces. The timbers are examined and numbered like an autopsy, and removed to another place. They pinpoint the building's date; a polished section's span of growth alternating in patterns that contain the secrets of past weather and enable the years to be measured in darkened, resinous rings.

'More than five hundred years of habitation in the body of this house, and nothing there now where it stood – water, just water. Little wind-driven inland waves lapping on the slippery shore, one tidemarked oak tree with its roots in wetness, and birdwatchers expectant with their telescopes, waiting to see what kind of life is there.'

3

House from Walderton, Sussex

ST CRISPIN'S DAY

It is the twelfth year of the sovereign reign of James. The house stands in the village down in the bottom fold at the mouth of the valley westwards below the fingers of Bow Hill, at a kink in the river Ems. Above the fields on the lower slopes, the sides of the Down are flanked with patches of yews and juniper and whitebeam. There have been settlements here for thousands of years; at the top of the ridge there are the lumps of tumuli, criss-crossing dykes, and the shallow, scraped remains of prehistoric flint mines.

Your sight of the house and what occurs in it is unclear, like straining to see movement behind a lattice of trees and branches in the blueness of dusk, or having one eye shut. You feel thwarted by the blindness, though there can be freedom in partial truths, a loosening of obligation to the unequivocal.

You can see that it is an old house, with hall and smoke and clay floor, and a keen draught blowing across the cross passage when both north and south doors are open to the garden. Inside, the blackened daub on the walls has worn away to a lizard shininess in places where the dishes and pails have been carried through from the buttery and knocked into the corner for a hundred years. John Catchlove is a husbandman of sixty-four years and you can read more of his last will and testament than he can himself.

'Can't read nor write because by the time the new vicar Diggens was teaching the children the English tongue I was nine years old and too big for lazing about on my sitting bones taking in nonsense that wouldn't get hay in or turnips dug.' And you can read perhaps half of the probate inventory of the goods he left to his daughters on his death in 1634:

Wearing apparel and money in his purse thirty shillings.

An iron pot.

A brass pot.

One saucer.

One spit.

Three tubs.

Two firkins.

One pair of pothangers.

One flitch of bacon.

Seven sheets.

The rest of the document is tattered and incomplete. But you can almost be sure that, during his lifetime, his wife cooks curd in the posnet, which they eat from the pewter or the wooden dishes, and that they sleep on the flock bed under three blankets, though you know that their dreams themselves are lost almost as quickly as they are encountered, and rarely if ever described to others, no matter how striking. You don't know if they sleep coiled together in the bed for warmth or comfort, or rigidly apart because amity gives rise to yet more children and Katherine and Martha are enough to feed, though he'd never begrudge them. You think that perhaps his uncle Thomas lives with him later, perhaps for sixteen years once he gives up farming, attempting odd jobs slowly about the house, his joints sore with age. You think he might keep bees in the North Garden or the half-acre of orchard, and that pippins are amongst the apples that he grows there too, going out in his ox-hide jerkin to thin out the clusters once the fruit is set. You are sure there are rooks wheeling above the house when the wind or a bold hawk disturbs the rookery in the beech hangar up on the hill, and you are sure that, during the Great Winter, the babies often cry with cold all night. You know he is buried in the month of May, and that any apple trees he has planted will go on yielding long after his demise.

The house, like anything else, is obscured by its own progress through time. Change happens in fits and starts and overlappings, after lulls and expectancy.

By the twenty-first year in the reign of Charles, it is being revised, repaired. Flint walls are built to encase the old oak timber-frame, with quoins at the corners made of brick. The proportions are sound and the house has a generous aspect to it. Ask any master builder or mason: 'If you want walls made in a workmanly fashion you'll need firm foundations. Good flint is freshly dug from the chalk before the brittleness has spoiled it, and when soft iron hammers can split it into quarters. You can see in the wall here that some flints have a white rind of chalk heel about them. I wouldn't be a flintknapper, it's a good enough wage they get but their chests are filled with dust they've breathed in before too long, and they die about thirty, thirty-five. Field flint is picked by children, when the young corn is finger-high and likes to be trampled on.'

When the house is nearly done by the end of August the reeders come with their waggonload of thatch.

'I did this job because when I climbed my father's ladder as a boy my head did not swim like my brother's did,' one thatcher says, 'and my hands soon grew very deft and strong, as they needed to. I can see more than most men can up here. I have a broad view of life.' He is tying bundles to the rafters with lengths of old man's beard soaked in a pail that a boy hands to him. When the bottom coat is done he'll lay on the weathering coat in long straw sparred with hazel. He winks. 'In the same way as they say you shouldn't squeeze a woman too hard, you don't lay the reeds too tight as it'll make a bad roof of it, sucking the water in when it pours down and not letting the wind in a bit to keep it dry.' The thatcher's skin is browned like fine gingerbread from being on rooftops all the season. He's always glad of the longer days and often works till after the sun's gone down, the dusk casting an grey-orange light over the backs of his hands and tools, when the jittering flecks of bats are about him. He can't work in winter, or when the long straw's wet.

The thatcher blinks in the sun. 'I work hard but I

look hard too,' he goes on. 'There's a lot to see up here, and I don't miss much. In that far orchard there's an old dame dragging a tub out to her chickens, and behind her there's a woman spreading a wet sheet out to dry on bushes. I can smell the dusty baked earth about the house where the builders have trodden for months. Behind me,' he points south, 'on the open Down I can hear the shepherd's flock. And skylarks, except for the thump of the legget when I'm dressing the last course of reeds into position. Nothing's more pleasing to the eye than a new crisp thatch all done and trimmed neatly.' The thatcher steadies himself with his knee against the angle of the north side of the roof, and takes another twist of bine from the boy.

Below on the lane a girl walks past, carrying her baby sister on her hip and whistling because she finds a tune always wheedles out of her when the sun is out. There is a musky smell of brambles, and clouds of thin flies bobbing in the heat.

'When we get home you can have a drink of well water,' she says, and rubs some dirt from the baby's fat, hot cheek.

Then the girl looks up, and she sees the thatcher's head shining yellow against the deep blue sky with the sun behind it, looking down, and the thatch is a sea of unfinished yellow too all about him, and the thatcher grins and gives a wave although he does not know her. And she smiles inside herself and considers that perhaps she does not glance upwards often enough, above the eaves and gable-ends and ridges. She has not thought such a thing before, and as she puts her mind to it more than a few times before the day is through, it jumps inside her.

'Keep your mouth closed when you chew,' her mother scolds sharply at supper, but the girl scarcely hears. She is deciding to walk that way past the piles of yealms in the yard tomorrow; right up to the door. 'Just to find out who's moving in when the house is done,' she murmurs aloud, though she's already sure and doesn't need to know that it's William Catchlowe.

William Catchlove
William Ketchlowe
William Cachelor, spell him how you will, must be pleased with his inheritance. He has secured a mortgage against the lease of the house to Mr Powell a tailor in West Dean, which has meant the refurbishment throughout the summer has been thorough and to a good standard. He derives particular satisfaction from the insertion of the new chimney in the middle of the house, heating not one but two chambers, and thinks that the addition of the bread oven in what he now terms the bake house on the western side, must be something close to brilliance. He stands in front of the unlit hearth, rocks on his heels on the ruddy bricked floor and swells with pride. He breathes in the smell of fresh workmanship and plaster, deeply. He runs both palms over the new sills and the lintel above the wide mouth of the hearth. He creaks up the stairs. He tests the hinges of the beech door into the upper chamber. He pictures the flock bed with its appurtenances and looks out of the glazed mullioned window to see if the eastern view up the valley has also changed as he feels himself to have done. He goes down to the cool service end of

the house and pictures the cheese presses, the treen, the sacks of flour, some Graffham pots. His fear of being buried under a heap of blackened, decaying timber that is held up with dust and cobwebs and God's will alone is fast diminishing, and the house feels as though it is unfurling, blooming, even as the mortar hardens against the approaching cold season.

'It was close to perishing where it stood. What I've done is no more extravagance than taking on the lease of a new field,' he says to himself boldly, as if rehearsing to counter the gossip that's flown around the parish about the twenty pounds he's spent, and his voice booms strangely in the empty room. 'It's thinking ahead, it's attending to what needs to be done, and doing it well. We have much to be grateful for, now the widespreading turmoil between citizens, God willing, has come to an end in this land.' He remembers to say a prayer of thanks, sweeps his hat upon his head and strides back up to Stoughton with the kind of firm and purposeful haste that comes from realising the objective of a lifetime. And it is most likely that his beer that night at the alehouse tastes exceedingly good, and that he ignores the disapproval of the few and orders jugs for the many, for does it not say in the Bible that a wise man builds his house solidly against the vagaries of weather?

After this date, there is a puzzling silence from the house that stretches for fifty cold years without clues or documents. But slowly, perhaps over several lifetimes, two mild hollows are worn into the brick paviors on the floor in the downstairs chamber. Whether by the rocking of two boots splayed akimbo before the fire, or the runners of a chair, or the dragging of frying pans and skillets by a housewife cooking, you will never know.

Time has sifted away all clues of this period inside the house; lost, rotted, crumbled, dried into dust, torn, or absorbed them back into itself, rubbed away all substantiation and proof. But this does not stop you from making hopeful lists of untruths and assumptions and piecemeal empathy to furnish the gaps, to redress the balance between what was and what might have been.

Like: perhaps the weather is harsh with hail and thunder all September.

Like: perhaps harvest is meagre and there is a comet.

Like: perhaps there are new taxes to pay, and parcels of land to negotiate for.

Or a woman's waters break and she has a stillborn, right there on the floor.

There is a glut of field fruits.

A widower dies they say of grief.

A father and son fight hand-to-hand over money and don't speak for a twelve-year.

On Easter eve a woman scorches her sleeves taking a cake from the oven.

There is a wedding and at the church door the bride bursts into tears and never says why for the length of her marriage which is forty-six years.

A woman lies in bed at night eaten up by jealousy.

New tenements are built over the way and an old one torn down.

A girl cooks a codling pie, then trips and breaks the

crust as she takes it to table.

The river Ems floods over and makes the wells dirty.

A man steals a ewe from his neighbour's flock, who never finds out who did it.

A parishioner does not attend church for the first time though a pious woman, much given to fasting.

An old woman goes mad and fills her store cupboard with nothing but stones.

A suckling calf is weaned from its mother.

Snow stays for weeks and the trees are an inky-brown blot against white, and a rare wild bird that nobody knows a name for is seen in the copse.

There is a plague of greenfly in the gardens.

A man enjoys a bit of ram's mutton for a change.

A man falls drunk in a ditch in daytime after selling a horse.

All of the skirrets are uprooted by badgers.

The road is mended.

A woman rocks backwards and forwards, feeding her third infant.

A man drives a pitchfork through his foot and his beard goes grey overnight.

A child slips off a cart and is headsick for months.

A pair of mallard freezes to death on the dewpond.

A boy makes a spoon.

A man tells a lie to his wife.

A youth oils a harness and traces.

A pig escapes.

A bolt rusts over on a door that is always kept shut.

It is curiosity, ghoulishness, passion that drives the

need to tell stories, whatever their consequence. And there are also a handful of incontestable facts to be found, without need for embellishment.

'Like the news that spreads in a flash on the night of the fire in Stoughton. The dreadful glow lights up the sky to the east of here for miles around. Stirred from their beds by shouts and disquiet, men run half-dressed right up the valley to help pull water from the Ems, mouths dry with agitation. Many houses are burnt to the ground and the vicarage razed, black ash and smuts and bits of blackened thatch rising and sinking and settling all over the remains of the village the next day, and an acrid burnt smell is left for weeks. Paupers are made on that night. It feels like divine wrath to me, and the faithful are put in fear. There are no non-conformists here, nor papists neither. We are a steady, rooted flock. But it is as though something profound is shaken by this occurrence, and the church declines without pause for fifty years, plummeting into disrepair. The east window is cracked, sparrows nest habitually at the back of the nave, and the north transept crawls with vermin, so that during the sermon it can be hard to fix upon the words of God lest a mouse run up your wife's petticoats.'

Tuesday, 3rd day in May, 1698. 'Today in the evening fell a great snow that lasted a few days, and a great frost froze up the land and shrivelled the crops. It is a disaster for those who rely on the earth's bounty this year, which is all of us.'

'You'll have heard of the smugglers? One of them

Edmund Richards from this parish – out at Long Coppice just up the way. The smugglers met in the forest last October being 1747, and broke into the customs house at Poole to seize all the tea there. Months later a gang (our man among them) went out and killed two men they said was informers. I can't say I know him though I've said good morning where we've crossed on the highway, a thickset man in a black frockcoat and neckerchief, kept himself to himself, and you can see why. No-one's seen him of late, or no-one says so. There's a warrant out but they've not apprehended him yet. Brutal it was, I'll spare you the details. Just think; the catkins all out in the hedgerows, the first buds of creamy primrose buttoning the banks and it was just after Valentine's. But let's say one ended buried alive in a foxhole at Harting, his hands over his face to have free of the dirt before he gasped his last, and the other not found till a dried-up corpse dragged out of a well by Edward Sone, in a horse pasture near Rowland's Castle, with his eyes gouged out. And some say they skinned their horses and had done with the meat to be rid of evidence. Such was the terror instilled by these brutes that not a soul ventured to mention anything of blood nor bodies, though several saw what it was that went on that night. Of course this week was the trial, and no-one's talking of much else in Walderton, and five of the gang to be hanged by the neck at the Broyle in Chichester and afterwards one of them swung in chains at Rook's Hill to soothe the populace. Won't catch me up in those woods by Long Coppice at dusk again not even after a fat brace of Stanstead game birds. Gives me the shivers, that kind of darkness under trees, like something of malice is watching you as you step along. I'd even think twice about going down to the trappers' bridge to get eels for supper, not till they've found him. Nothing's safe in this world, mind you I've always held how tea is a dangerous drink.'

Thursday, 19th day in April, 1759. 'There is a clean rain coming down outside and I, John Tripp, cannot look at it without thinking of the new crops drinking it in, each green ear of wheat or barley starting to swell with a milky sap. From today I must begin to pay my rent instead to a baker in Westbourne. I do not think it will alter anything.' He fetches his hook, and a whetstone and strap with which to sharpen it; and when the rain is over he ventures out to cut furze on the hill. He goes up Down Lane, turning to take the view from time to time whilst gaining height. 'And I am presently rewarded,' he says, 'by the sight of the foot of a rainbow arching above the green hill opposite, somewhere between Brocksnap and Bottom Field. A yellowhammer flits to the top of a wild service tree before me and breaks into such reedy hoarse insistence that I am obliged to pause further to admire it too, so that I am greatly startled by a noise which at first I think is a broken wheel on the stony track behind me, but which proves to be a beggar, clapping the lid of his wooden alms-dish as he comes round the corner. Forlornly clad in a torn coat soaked through, no hat at all upon his greasy head, and with one shoe bound together with a bit of rag, he garbles out some words as he advances. "I humbly beg you take pity on a poor wretch reduced in circumstances, sir, spurned by his own parish, I can see you have a Christian heart of charity, sir, spare me some trifle towards the common necessaries of life, a little half-groat or farthing." I give him tuppence though it will leave me short. It could be many of us living parlously in that way given a misfortune or two strung together, taking cover in barns with the rats, eating stolen eggs and turnip tops set out for pigs to feed upon. I am thankful for the roof above my head, and the three silvery planks of the oak door that stand firm after nightfall between my mortal self and the uncertain world out there.'

In 1793 the building is in use as a poorhouse. You know nothing of it; whose straitened circumstances cause them to be here, or for how long. But you can picture flashes of likeliness:

'Sir and gentlemen of the parish of Stoughton. Great distress I am compelled to write. Cannot undertake to pay house rent. Have scarce a bit of bread. Husband suffering under his old complaint and has fits of late. Our insufficiency of supporting these four children. Still in hopes through God's goodness.'

A girl in her underskirt mending the hem of a shabby green gown with a strip of cloth.

A mother wiping the innards of pots with a piece of shared bread so that nothing is wasted.

A widower cold in the bed at night.

A man breaking the fire up to save fuel for the morning.

A row of children with their eyes fixed on the spoon's movement as porridge is served.

However, in 1837, Thomas Lowe who owns the

house divides his legacy between his children, leaving the daughter the half of the cottage which lies to the east and the son the other that lies to the west. The bisection is as even-handed as it can be. 'And the washhouse is to be shared, which means that our paths cross often enough. You will see that we do not share a chimney.'

In this way a clearly descending line of first-born sons called Thomas Mills inherit the eastern side of the house, one after the other, over the span of more than a hundred years. They are in turn cordwainer, bootmaker, master shoemaker; and the shoemakers' shop to the north of the house has the good, warmly pungent smell of new leather and boiled resin as part of its fabric, as does Thomas Mills about his person.

'At least I know my spirit won't go barefoot after death, for there have been some who have not paid me for their shoes,' he asserts. 'It takes a week to make four pairs of boots or thereabouts. Cut to the foot's measurement on the board with the clicking knife, the uppers are closed then pulled over the last with the pincers once the heel stiffeners and toe are put in. The holes for thread are drilled out, then the uppers, welt and sole are stitched together using both ends of thread; a cobbler's stitching is not unlike flying in his movements. The heels are nailed on in lifts, and shaved.

'I have a lap stone, a stirrup, a burnishing iron, sewing awls, a hammer, a sleeker, sometimes apprentices, and also a tame cock linnet to keep me company when my wife is too busy with her domestic duties to wax the hemp for me, unless I've got a rush job on. I hang

the bird's cage outside the door on a fair day, and find
its twittering helps a man summon up the magic of his
work at the ends of his fingers, which in the finest pairs I
would describe as the making of a second skin to clothe
the foot, if that's not too fancy a notion. But I'm not
saying that's what always happens at the bench. Out on
the verges of Cooks Lane there is a little grass vetchling
that they call shoes-and-stockings for the shape of the
scarlet flowers, but there's some years I've known it to
never show its face.'

Speaking of vegetable growth and flora, you are
reminded that some say that the very first Victoria plum
comes from a garden in Walderton. This is a fruit that
seems to have caught a piece of the shine of the sun
itself in its waxy orb. It shares this soil with russet apples,
pearmains. A man could resent giving up a tenth of his
glorious fruit to the rector. He'd rather the wasps ate
them, he thinks, standing still in the orchard. There's
the noise of sawing up at George Hedgecock's place,
and a baby bawling. Beyond the trees he can see the
dot of a person on horseback taking the bridle road to
Chichester over the Down. At least now it is a tithe in
money that he gives up with the rent at Lady Day and
Michaelmas, not the good plums themselves.

'You'll see reminders of things all round the
fireplace. Those corner bricks on the right; worn away
where I've whetted my pocket knife for years. The
hearth is the core of any dwelling, the place of warmth
and confluence, and if the dead do return, no doubt this
would be the place they come to. So if you see, out of

the corner of your eye as you enter a room, a shadow bent over the fire as if turning the coals, trying to get warm, then perhaps it is only to be expected − or it could be the smoke.

'My brother who's dead now sat in that chair. We've paid him a year's-mind lately at church and the vicar did an exemplary sermon that day, but that he's still fresh in our heads and our hearts is the truth. George always took that chair right by the fireside, with his legs crossed wearing the boots I'd made for him, leaning to tap out the bowl of his clay pipe against the grate. And my nephew George who was named for him and baptised the month that we laid my brother in the ground, lived only two short months of this life and was buried by December. My wife Mary Ann was cruelly big with child though we didn't know then how blessed we were. My brother John was deeply grieved at his double loss, and we felt great sorrow for him seven years later when his little boy William lasted but five days before slipping from this world. My brother John mostly gave up shoemaking for working the land as a labourer because he could not bear to be indoors. He said it made his head ache, sitting inside the gloom of the house all day, hunched over the bench banging holes into leather for other folk's feet. He wanted to have the wind on his skin, to fall into bed at night with his limbs exerted, to feel the annular way of things. Our twins Frank and Fanny were born thriving the next year and were baptised at Whitsun.'

The western side of the house, once old Mrs Lowe dies in 1876, you find increasingly hard to understand in terms of occupancy. There are mires of names in lists and contradictions: James Stenning, Louisa McBain, you cannot tell whether Gaffer Mills the blacksmith ever lived in the house that he owned. Neither can you believe all you read of the house, because some of it is impossible. Even the recent past can become impenetrable again; little shreds of the wrong information tangled together. It is as though the neglect that will happen later to this part of the house infects it backwards in time from this point onwards, obscuring its visible history from view as if with weeds and the abrupt bristle of undergrowth that takes hold when it can. You are as far from it as anything else that you do not know.

In the eastern side of the house, someone is fond of wallpaper; a restless taste that often needs refreshing with a new design. Perhaps the fondness starts with Mary Ann Mills, once the children are grown and she has less on her hands all of a sudden, and when her husband begins to draw his salary as postal officer of Walderton. In the post office, things converge between sender and receiver. There are red stamps, lilac. Not much is clear about the wallpaper, neither about its dates nor extent inside the parlour, so that you do not know when to imagine the first of the seventeen layers was put up, how large an area it covered, nor how long an interval between each was decently left.

'I'm making paste for the hanging. Half-quartern of flour mixed with clean cold water in a pail till it's like cream, then take the kettle from the hob and pour on boiling water, stirring all the while until it thickens, then stand it by until quite cold. Mrs Mills finds the reek of paste as it goes off too disagreeable, so put in crystals of carbolic acid dissolved in warm water. It does no harm and sees off the cockroaches.

'She's fed up with the earthy shades of last time – buff and creamy leaves and curlicues stamped on over the colour of pots. She finds it a bit sickly, she says, day in day out. I like this new pale one myself that's going on top, though it's clearly a lady's paper, small and chintzy with olive-green tendrils and geranium flowers, and it suits the room. Though it was way back, I remember the first was a shocker; the darkness of dried blood with larch-green prints of something like leaves creeping up and up the walls. When it was done, on stepping in here the air felt stuffy to breathe even if the window was propped open. I couldn't help think it must be like the colour of bad dreams you'd have if you'd spent days killing livestock by lamplight. But I didn't say that to her as she seemed pleased with it and asked Mrs Benford over to drink tea with her right away once it was hung. There's no doubt it looked very genteel, despite the bumps and unevenness of wall I'd had to contend with.'

1891. 'Walking down Breakneck Lane early of an evening after work, I'm smelling the victuals women are preparing with their ranges stoked up, and all the good odours going up the chimneys and mingling in the air. I can catch maybe dumplings, bacon; there are frying smells of butter which could be griddle cakes, and the bitter, boggy smell of cabbage. Mostly it's meat that a working man craves, and a bit of bacon with mustard is never amiss.

'I pass Malthouse Cottages and Rhoda Russell comes out and tips a tub of soapy water into the mead to drain into the river, and straightens up to see who it is on the road, her hair in her eyes. She's getting old now to be lifting heavy vessels up like that but being a widow she sometimes has a bit of laundry in still – there's always people who need things washed. Abreast of the Lambourn's place I pass the rector and he raises his soft, Godly hand to me as he glides by on his bicycle. And as I come towards the Barley Mow past the post office I can hear on either side of the road the Mills's tapping away at those boots with their hammers. Things are looking up in a place when there's enough trade to keep two cobblers in business. The hips are bright in the hedge; and, up on the Down, mistle thrushes are gorging on yew berries. Later I sit and have a read of the Weekly Advertiser. Terrible to think of all those people in Russia, starving to death.'

In 1930, the last occupant of the western half of the cottage leaves for good. Then the war starts, and the unwholesomeness of neglect lasts throughout its duration. When it rains the drumming on the tin roof that has replaced the thatch is deafening, and there are leaks, mice, the threat of vandals.

During the night of the Dieppe raid in August 1942, two bombs are dropped on the village.

During the Battle of Britain a Molotov breadbasket of eleven incendiary bombs falls beside cottages, but no-one is hurt and there is little damage.

A granary takes a direct hit, bursting into flames,

so that for a long time afterwards the breakfast smell of toast reminds many people in Walderton of charred grain and anxiety and the sight of a sky that is lit up with crimson, smouldering flames feeding on wheat.

In September a fighter pilot crashes in Stoughton, killing the pilot who is Polish.

In spring 1944, inexplicable white lines are painted on roads for vehicular activity. No visitors are permitted into the area.

The war ends.

There are many former things left over from the way the world was before the war. But choosing shoes to wear on the Feast of St Crispin and St Crispianus is one of the many serious matters that old Thomas Mills will not have to think of again. It is fitting that a shoemaker dies during the time dedicated to his patron saint. And in 1946, the year of his passing aged eighty-five, St Crispin's Day is cloudy and mild, with showers of rain followed by spells of sunshine that brighten the leaves – just the usual weather for October. There is a brisk wind from the southeast that is calm by the evening, and the ribby wood has settled into a steadier leaf fall. The yellowed blackthorn is clinging to its little spears of leaf, so transparent they seem almost alight with the light from the white sky.

In the post office, David Mills notes the arrival of the Festival of Britain commemorative stamp.

Watching the building come down in 1980, you see it is mapped, filmed, made into plans, squared up and measured with lengths of string. The excavation plans of the floors are meticulous maps of the unknowable; burnt areas, green clay, brown clay, yellow mortar, puddled chalk. It's early summer; the group picks adroitly through the building in shirtsleeves, making notes and numbers with each layer as it comes away. The air is grassy, dusty, friable, as though the house has suffered inexplicable drought. The timbers are wrapped and stacked up like an extraordinary raft. The thatch is clouds of dissected stuff, ripped up and thrown down in choking armfuls to the ground. And, watching this, it occurs to you that perhaps some parts of the past have no use, like the packing that protects an interesting object in transit.

The dismantling of so much useful history takes just three weeks to complete.

4

Gonville Cottage at Singleton, Sussex

HOME

Revolutions are brewing all over Europe when Gunfield Cottage goes up in 1847 – Germany, Prussia, Austria.

An overcast day with no rain to speak of, and Richard Burns is already out with his sheep on the Down; his dog's a bobtail, the rough-haired sort. The house is tiny below him; a squarely-built dot beside the sheepyard behind trees in the green valley that runs from West Dean to Singleton and beyond.

He catches a ewe with his crook round its hind leg, pulls brambles from the coat and lets it go. 'The Southdown's a good breed. Bears the cold well, and close-wooled – thick and curdled with a good depth of staple. Though it's a light carcass, say twenty pounds per quarter, it yields a good weight of flesh compared to others on land of the same value, and it's the herbage that makes the breed tasty.' He nods at the edge of the flock. 'They don't have a rambling disposition, though I like to put bells on them. Those that are white-faced are the good milkers.'

He has read about the Chartists in the Sussex Chronicle and though he knows that so far he has been dealt a fair card in life, he has seen others crushed and gets satisfaction from hearing of thousands in outright protest. 'For the working man,' he thinks aloud, 'things could be different.' He gets his wage half-yearly, and the house comes with the work, and he's free to trap all the rabbits he can eat – so long as he doesn't rub that in the face of Charlie Boxall the gamekeeper, though it's none of his business. Going to work with cold rabbit pie in your dinner bag with the pocket knife and tin of fly-powder makes the rain less wet, though there's no denying how slippery the chalkpath gets.

Like most shepherds he doesn't say much, and most words he utters are likely as not to his flock. He has noticed how, as with some family members, there are some sheep that appear to listen more closely than others. He rarely has cause to question his faith in the firmness of things, but knows that each month presents its own trouble. 'People see a shepherd sitting out with his flock of maybe three hundred, and they see a man doing nothing wearing a dog-hair hat and oilskin cape in the drizzle. What they can't see is how he's keeping an eye out for the ewes and the wethers. There's plenty to watch for: stiffness of legs, foxes, redwater, dropsy, rot, flux. Charlock's a poison just growing amongst crops. There's adders, thieves.'

At the end of the day he gathers them back down off the hill and they pour into the fold on Greenways Field that's in rotation for wheat. He checks the hurdles are sound and even as he enters the house, his ears are still trailing the bleats as they settle.

He props his crook next to the spare crook-sticks made of hazel that he's seasoning in the corner. This room downstairs opposite the kitchen is given over to shelves of things that he needs for tending through the year; like the ruddle pots, tailing irons, ear punches, dipping hooks, shears in pouches, canister bells and cluckets, lambs' bottles with teats, and scraps of emery paper to clean his best crook bright for sheep fairs like Findon. On fair day he has to start driving them at two in the morning to get there for six. There's rabbit wires hanging on a nail, and a old white overcoat that's waterproofed in boiled oil, and a green umbrella, four foot across with whalebone ribs. It's nice to see his wife. She pours some black tea that's been brewing on the hob.

The house is not meanly-built. Flint-faced with four double-square windows overlooking the sheepyard, a hoop-chip thatch. There are two other cool, dark rooms at the back; a scullery and pantry. There's a privy to the rear, and two bedrooms upstairs. He doesn't notice the smell which pervades everything here; sharp-sweet dung and lanolin.

'Lambing time I'll come in for a bit of peace but the house is full of their noise. You can't think for the bleating. It gets in your head, that million-fold quavering, it's all you can hear, and it pulls at your insides so you can't sleep more than a snatch at a time, like having infants. Lambing is hardest – mid-spring there's some nights I don't get more than a wink, in and out of that yard with the horn lamp lit through all the hours of darkness. They don't like fuss, ewes, but they need seeing over. A lamb being born, it slithers out. Not like the birth of my daughters – those women wouldn't let me in but I could hear the screaming. No – here it's no trouble when it's going well, just a steaming lamb suddenly on the straw in the chill air, glistening with newness and wetness in the yellow light's span.

'And because the lambing fold is by the house I can glance up coming back from the straw stump to scatter fresh litter in the hurdle pens. If a light's on in the bedchamber I know Fanny or Mary is woken or my wife's legs are bad and she's rubbing on liniment. First year we were here Mother was still with us too and her rheumatic affliction at eighty-four meant she had to sleep downstairs till the cold day she died. Dr Turner was an expense. When a ewe's coupling up, with the lamb on its legs and suckling, she gets a swede or mangel pronged out of the heap for her. Come the mornings I rake out the soiled bedding before it gets hot and thick which gives them lameness in their feet.

'Tupping is six weeks' hard work for me and the dog come November, when the ewes get gathered once a day to the ram to be served. Dipping is end of August – closing the watergate halfway to West Dean to build up the water, fencing the road off and driving them down. They've got to be three minutes in water, swimming upstream after they're scrubbed. I might have a jar at the Horse and Groom afterwards. I do that a fortnight before shearing, to let the natural yolk rise again in the fleece, about midsummer, say, though if it's fat stock a bit earlier. The shearing gang comes up from Sidlesham, each man doing forty to fifty sheep a day. There's a lot of beer gets drunk, there's twenty fleeces to a tod. It's the finest for broadcloth, after Welsh.

'Fodderwise, the tegs get some hay on frosty mornings, and the rest they forage for themselves, except in the heart of winter when they get cake and corn. Come early summer I take them up that narrow white bostal path to the side of the Trundle, as the valley grass is over-rich by then. They need a firm footing when they can and the wool is better up on a sheep walk – too much pasturing makes it coarse and heavy. I don't mind being up there, those months. You can see toadflax, fleawort, blue butterflies, field crickets.

'They get folded at night. After harvest they don't go up so much, there's grazing on stubble, and the winter there's also root crops like turnips. Some have tried potatoes for the winter, sliced up in the troughs – I know there's plenty to be bought from Chilgrove way but they're a funny tasteless vegetable and it's neither natural fodder nor tried and tested.

'Ewe lambs are better if brought up frugally. It's the ram lambs and wethers that need more attention, feeding and management. But actual daughters – they're far more flummoxing to instil obedience into, because they reshape themselves all the time, so that a man can't keep a hold of what their sense is. My Olive, at school she was a source of paternal pride to me, applying herself to needlework and cyphering and looking after the house when it helped her poor mother. Things have changed so. In the same way that you can sense when a hazard's approaching up in the field even before you can see or smell it, I can sense some kind of trouble might be nearing us; she's become a saucy girl who won't do as I say like she used to. Gone are the days when I could send her off up the woods with a bucket to gather snails to feed the pig, and now she's earning wages for herself down at Binderton she won't bend her will to mine. There's not much to do after feeding them and keeping them clean and in boots and giving them a fear of God and the way to do good by him. My daughters have had a start in life, when you think of some sending their children off to learn at school with nothing but cold raw turnip in their bellies, and others not to school at all. Home – what is that if it's not a place to set root in the ground awhile?

'If a man of politics was to come here and ask me what I thought of the worth of common men who work by the land, well if it's not immodest I'd mention I've won a few prizes for raising sheep to high standards. But would it be asking too much to be given the vote?' Richard Burns does not know.

'Have to respect your animals, but I'm not soft about it. To some people naming no names they are live money walking on legs. When they look at them they must be thinking of their parts broken down, like a master-butcher's chart, into fat quarters and offal – which is head, horn, feet, innards, pluck, blood and pelt. They're not great tallowers. But why would you think of that on a fine day like this with the parkland looking so green and the young trees beginning to take a hold after the planting. Sheep've mostly a right to a good life, though ruptured or bad-uddered ewes are put to cull. Mid-winter day is the day for slaughter, and then butcher them on Christmas Eve. Southdown wether-mutton is the best sort, fine grained, and they say with a delicacy of flavour. But there it is.'

Olive Burns is sixteen. She has gone to pick watercress on her way to visit home on Sunday afternoon from Preston Farm where she's in service – sometimes it's nice to have something to take back to them all, apart from her house-maid's wages and gossip for her sisters. The far side of Binderton is a soggy, green place, oozing in mid-spring with fresh water bubbling up from springs under the ground to join the river Lavant.

'"Just one more little bit," I'm saying though there's none to hear me, so that I can tolerate the cold about my ankles. I'm almost laughing trying to bear it. "One handful torn from here, and then I'm done." Little marsh frogs are jumping everywhere I step. There's strings of weed, I've got my hems tucked up out of the water, and then round the corner comes William Grainger who's finished in the field, and I can feel my face burn up in case he overheard me talking to myself like a mad old cow.

'"Why don't you come out of that Olive Burns and sit and talk to me?" he shouts across. I think this is a very bold way to speak to a girl he scarcely knows.

'"I'm in a hurry," I shout back, looking at the water as if to check for frogs. I am stuck in the water and can't come out as my legs are bare and my feet all red with the chill. The water is icy cold here – you have to take cress from a place where you know it's clean. And then he's gone, just like that, and I'm struggling to put my stockings back on my wet feet in a hurry in case he comes back and sees I've a wet patch on the back of my gown. Silly to be so ruffled about it I keep saying all the way home.'

'"What's with you?" Mary says crossly as I walk in.

She doesn't get enough fresh air since Eliza got married because she's indoors looking after our mother. Doing the jobs Mother can't do; the washing, starching, bluing, cooking, mostly everything that needs being done. If she goes out it's in a rush to fetch tea, pork, candles, or to church on Sundays. Mother's bad at the moment, it pains her hips even to stand or walk a few steps. When we pick her up she's like a birdcage. I worry she'll fall down those stairs and break her legs one day. It's like her bones are as dry as tinder.

'When I was a girl I would run up on the grass to pick rampions and speedwell, and bee orchids and burnet rose. The furze-jacks would be twittering in the bushes and you could see blue wheatears' eggs laid right inside rabbit holes. There's no time for that anymore.

'How did I end up getting wed to Billy Grainger? Well, how does anyone – it happens and that's that. Reverend Bowles gave me a speech about how I wasn't a maiden in the sight of God. But you've got no proof now. People tutting and shaking their heads, never looking me quite in the eye as though they might catch something from me. Hardly the first.' She shrugs. 'Love? You don't have to go digging for it you know. Gives them something to talk about is all.'

And you do not know whether she bore a child or miscarried one, because there is no more sight of Olive Burns or her fate to be had.

1859. It's the year Richard Burns leaves the house to move into the village and the northern lights are brightly visible in the night sky for over a week.

'Sunday night must be the most lovely,' somebody's

mother says, 'like a giant fox tail brushing the sky.'

From February of any year there is the quick noise of the river Lavant as it starts up its flowing through the lower fields, and then come spring there's a spreading-out silence and wetness when the sluices are opened and the water meadows glisten. You see a heron slow-stalking in the field for worms. By July the riverbed is dry again.

You know that sometimes the house is empty now, and sometimes it's not.

A man greases his hair back with lard, getting ready for church. In the back room he can hear his wife complaining about how fast their boy is getting taller. 'And his chilblains are swelled up so bad he can't get his boots on as his feet have grown so.'

One St Roche's Day, which is the 16th of August, there is a thick grey fog rolled in off the sea from Pagham Harbour, and there is a lot of talk about the devil being buried up there on the Trundle, and of dogs heard barking. 'It's not the devil up on St Rook's, more like the spirit of a murderer called Benjamin Tapner whose bones they say were buried where they fell rotting from the gibbet over a hundred years past, which was no doubt no more than he deserved.'

By 1871, out in the garden by the well, you think that perhaps Elizabeth Pratt is bringing the washing in with her daughter. It is chilly and almost dusk, and the damp sheets and pinafores are pale in the gloom and smell of soap. Pheasants have gone to roost in the chestnut trees beside the track.

'I need to ask Dadda something,' Lottie might say.

'Your father's not back yet,' her mother answers, shivering. 'Hold the bag for the pegs.'

'Mamma?' Lottie looks up. Her eyes are catching the fleck of candlelight from the open cottage door, as though a deep thought were suddenly lit inside her head. 'How can a ladybird be cold of body when it's so fiery hot in colour?'

'Don't know about that,' she replies. 'Just fold those up quickly and we can go in.'

'But they say it at school,' she persists, and sounds so anxious that Elizabeth Pratt bursts out laughing.

'There are many questions, little one, that I can't answer!' And she puts down the creaking weight of the basket to swing her daughter high against the sky, so that the whole valley's width of blackness hangs beneath her. Her own mother would have called her feckless; doing things on a whim, smiling too much and humming hymns as she goes back to the cluttered kitchen to get the dinner on.

Joseph Pratt is probably still at work, clearing roots on the edge of the woods up at West Hat Down near the big ruined house, stoking the last of a bonfire with the smoke drifting eastwards. It is likely he knows in what month the dog's mercury will be shimmering its mass of green under the beech trees, and where to look for a fat, pinkish pigeon, or where to find teasels. He knows that sparrowhawks swallow smaller birds whole after cutting off the beak, and that the only time to cut rods for hurdles is when the sap is down. He does not know how to read and write. He does not know that next year his wife Lizzie will die after the birth of their ninth child Henry, nor that in ten years time his son James will be a soldier.

Down on the road you can hear a horse going over the humpback bridge. It might be Violet the fourteen-hand strawberry mare from Singleton Farm. She'll be sold at the sale there in 1892, with the rest of the stock – the reaping machine, the stump of mixed hay, the linseed cake, the saddles, the oat-bin, the harrowing chains, the one sack of barley-meal. But it's early morning; it might be Albert Chalk driving the churns on the milkcart to Singleton Station.

Women plant potatoes on the side of Lamb Down.

Another weathering coat of straw goes on the thatch.

George Webb lives at the house for two years, packs up his brickmaking gear and goes again.

A train's whistle shrills. During Goodwood race week, the village teems as it always does with men and horses.

A shooting party in the Park kills a thousand pheasant in a day, the gundogs running back and forth across Long Barradine Field and the Garston. That night behind the house there is a sunset the colour of chalk and apricots.

A woman sits in a tin tub by the fire – the bathwater milky with Sunlight soap and scum. When she is done her husband swills it out at the backdoor drain, or it goes on the marrows.

The second world war comes.

From up on the hill in 1940 you see Portsmouth glowing as shells burst over the city. In April the next year you can see planes coming down. Four years later you hear the buzz of a doodle bug suddenly stop, and after the silence as its engine cuts out it explodes in the beechwoods right by the house but no one is hurt. After this the children don't protest about wearing their gas masks; it's only the dusty rubber smell they don't like.

There are less sheep now, as much of the Down has been ploughed up for crops. And the low-flying planes are causing distress with the flocks – ewes should never be made uneasy as it causes them to slip their lambs.

A bomb falls on Cucumber Farm one night. It kills or maims most of Reg Stay's herd of heifers.

'The noise is hideous,' Reg Stay says; up on the hill in the blackout, groping to find them to shoot them out of their misery, coming home all drenched in blood, weeping. 'Like butchery it is.' Reg Stay hears their squealing for years afterwards.

Later you stand with families watching a wide skyful of planes and gliders stream over in thousands going to France, the air is thick with them to east and west as far as the eye can see.

Men begin to come home with their minds blown to pieces.

In 1957 the Lavant floods, and the winter wheat is ruined in Bury Field.

An old man, whose breath smells of gently decomposing melons, is bent over his vegetable patch as he digs up artichokes. 'Home?' He thinks carefully and turns a forkful of earth. 'It's where the living thing inside you becomes knotted with a place, for however long.' He stares at the loam. 'It's where you come from but also where you go to.' He shakes the fork. 'It's where you stand in the graveyard and know the names on too many headstones. It's where the smell of grief for what's gone combines with your hope for what is to come.' He slides the pale knobbled artichokes onto the grass, in fours and fives. 'It's seeing a light in the window after a long journey. It's opening the gate, putting a hand on the latch, calling out to someone inside. It's being inside and waiting for someone to arrive.' The old man looks up at the face of the house.

The prevailing wind comes from the southwest.

In the woods, boys roll mortar shells down the hillside and put bullets left over from the war into their trouser pockets.

Later a man paints the living room green.

There is an infestation of ladybirds.

Another man cuts a hole in the door for a catflap, plants purple honesty and shrubs, arum lilies, raspberry canes. He puts up a greenhouse, a bird table. He moves out.

The paintwork is redone in a creamy gloss for a family, a dimplex heater fitted in the bathroom, new tiles. The kitchen cupboard fills with bits of homework, stickers, gardening gloves, receipts from the supermarket, pay slips, boxes of cereal.

By the time the family leaves, the noise of the traffic has grown overnight into a wall of sound – commuters, tourists, the rumble of lorries going up to the oilfield.

Undisturbed in the overgrown garden, pigeons tear at beakfuls of buds on the elder.

The sun is out.

Your lengthening shadow is very distinct now, and you see that it could be the shape of anyone, stepping over the threshold. And you find that a house that is waiting has a particular smell – the kind that twists at memories of home that you might recall from a long time ago, but are losing the words for.